Carrots, Peas, Spinach and Tomatoes, Broccoli, Lima Beans, Corn, and Potatoes!

Written by Karra Barber Wada

Illustrations by Thomas Barber

Dedicated To

Cali Cove and Kru Coast Wada

Happy Reading!

"It's time for supper"
Mama Dog yelled,
"Big Dog, Small Dog,
even Little Pupper!"

Wash your paws
and wipe your faces,
grab a spoon,
and take your places.

Carrots, Peas, Spinach, and Tomatoes,
Broccoli, Lima Beans,
Corn, and Potatoes.

These are the vegetables
in Mama Dog's soup.
They're different shapes and sizes,
and all good for you.

Orange, green,
yellow, red and brown,
lots of different colors,
grown from the ground.

Carrots, Peas, Spinach, and Tomatoes,
Broccoli, Lima Beans,
Corn, and Potatoes.

Big Dog growled
and said to them all,
"Eat your vegetable soup,
it makes you strong and tall."
But Little Pupper couldn't
EAT… ONE… BITE… AT… ALL.

Small Dog shouted,
look at my bowl,
the soup filled my tummy,
and tasted good and yummy.

Poor Little Pupper
wanted his supper.
He sat at the table,
but just wasn't able.

Mama Dog pleaded,
"EAT, EAT, EAT!"
But poor Little Pupper,
would just rather sleep.

Big Dog, Mama Dog, and Small Dog alike
were all very worried
about Pupper's appetite.
Or was it….. the vegetables he didn't like?

All of a sudden,
Pupper's tummy began to growl.
He was hungry for Mama's soup,
he started to howl.

Carrots, Peas, Spinach, and Tomatoes,
Broccoli, Lima Beans,
Corn, and Potatoes.

All these vegetables
are good for the tummy.
Pupper will tell you
they taste good and yummy.

9 798330 617814